THE OFFICIAL GUMBALL 3000

...own as the 'Daytona' because of Ferrari's overwhelming victory in the Daytona endurance ...ce in the late 1960's.

Max Speed (mph)	173
0-60 (seconds)	6.1
Max Power (bhp)	352

Entered under the name of 'Team Texas', this RUF reached its top speed on more than one occasion whilst on home territory!

Max Speed (mph)	
0-60 (seconds)	

Full-blast power and devilish good looks that strike ...ts hearts of even the bravest of men.

	17
	4.6
	38
	14
	799
	$68,82
	14.5
	65

Venturi Trophy 400 GT

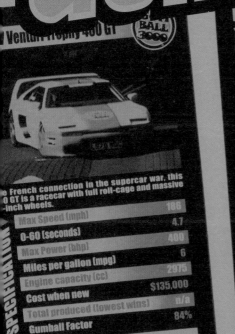

...e French connection in the supercar war, this ...0 GT is a racecar with full roll-cage and massive ...-inch wheels.

1999   Runs on onions and garlic!

2002 Noble M12 GTO - 3

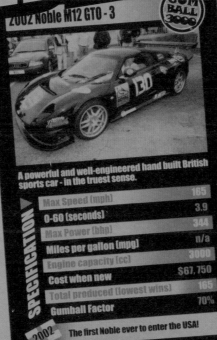

A powerful and well-engineered hand built British sports car - in the truest sense.

2002   The first Noble ever to enter the USA!

2002 Aston Martin DB7 Vantage Volante

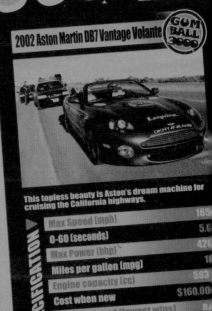

This topless beauty is Aston's dream machine for cruising the California highways.

2002   "Sir, could you show me your driver's licence and I-D".

...5 Ferrari 512M

...512M was the latest incarnation of the 'Testarossa' ...acy.

2001 Lamborghini Diablo 6.0 VT

The latest and greatest of the Diablo series.

1998 Ferrari F355 GTS

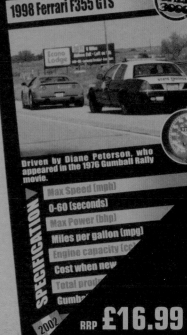

Driven by Diane Peterson, who appeared in the 1976 Gumball Rally movie.

2002

RRP **£16.99**

Title: Gumball 3000 The Annual
Sub Title: 2003 Rally
www.gumball3000.com

ISBN 0-9547226-0-4
EAN 9 780954 722609

Published by:
Gumball 3000 Merchandise Limited
4, Lucerne Mews,
London
W8 4ED
Great Britain

First published 2004

Produced By: Duncan Scholes
Executive Producer: Maximillion Cooper
◆ Design and Art Direction: Karen Jane (www.karenjane.com)
Text: Chris Quigley, Photo Edit: Leon Chew
Cover; Main image: Leon Chew (chew.tv) Car insert: Nick Thomson, Girl insert: Eyhab Jumean
Illustrations pages; 12, 22, 64, 84, Guy Passey (guy.passey@virgin.net)
Illustrations pages; 76, 90, by Geri Ford (www.rawshark.net)
Printed in the UK by Butler and Tanner

THE OFFICIAL ANNUAL 2004
GUMBALL 3000

CONTENTS

This Annual Belongs To: ....../.a.n............

Would you like to be Burt?
Simply cut around the dotted
line to become Burt Reynolds!

GUMBALL 3000

WELCOME RACE FANS!

"On a clear day in April, 145 cars from around the world assembled in San Francisco for an event which has rapidly entered international motoring mythology. For the next six days these cars will drive and party across America to Miami in an event that combines grease, glamour and guts in equal measure.

The Gumball is a modern day version of the infamous 70's road trip movies – and its present day cast includes everyone from the famously well off to the avid car enthusiast.

The attraction of the rally transcends social barriers. The appeal is to the adventurer in all of us, regardless of status or wealth. For many it's a chance to forget everything and indulge their passion for the machine that changed the world, the motorcar.

Now in its fifth incarnation, this is the second time the rally has taken place in America.

The Gumball 3000 is about to begin, so fasten your seat belts and start your engines please..."

Above: The now coveted Spirit of the Gumball bronze bust trophy of Burt Reynolds...

Maximillion's passion for 'motor racing', 'fashion' and 'music' began at an early age undoubtedly under the influence of family submerged in motoring history and tradition, combined with having a rock 'n' roll father who bashed the drums for a living. Entrepreneurial symptoms of 'buying and selling' cars (for ludicrously high profits!) and raising sponsorship money for F1 teams whilst studying a Fashion Degree at London's St. Martins College led to an ambition to create the 'most fashionable, rock 'n' roll' and notorious' car event ever.

In 1999 Maximillion invited 50 of his closest friends and acquaintance's, from 'rock stars to royalty', to take part in a crazy 3000 mile race around Europe, with the wildest parties each evening. In capturing the attention of the world's media, it was certain that Gumball would develop into something bigger. Having conquered the US over the past two years, and gracing the covers of Fortune 500 and GQ magazine, Max is on course to take 'Gumball 3000' further on its quest for global take over. As far as Empire building, making movies, designing clothes and launching boutiques, he has only just begun...

GUMBALLER PROFILE:

Name:

MAXIMILLION COOPER

Age: 31
Nationality: British
Home Town: London
Occupation: Gumball Founder
Career highlights: Ex-British Ping Pong Champion

Make of car driven in the Gumball: 2003 Lamborghini Murcielago

Special modifications: Broken electric windows

Q&A:

What is your ultimate Gumball car?
A pimped out white Rolls-Royce Phantom with white Gucci leather interior, 26" Chromes and a bottle of Cristal chilling in the Refrigerator!

What's your daily ride?
A 1969 Lotus Type 47 'Gulf Oil' race car

What's your favourite car related movie?
Bullitt

What's your favourite music?
The Clash

What's your favourite clothing brand?
Gucci

What's your favourite magazine?
Grand Royal

Who is your greatest hero of all time?
James Hunt

What's the most outrageous thing you've ever done?
Got married and had 2 beautiful daughters in the space of 3 years (its also the best thing I've ever done!)

What was your worst moment on the Gumball?
On the 2000 Rally trying to convince the owners of two Russian aeroplanes to take off without having paid for them.

What was your best moment on the Gumball?
Proposing to my wife on the 2001 rally and her accepting!

Who from history would be your dream Gumball co-driver?
Steve McQueen

Sum up your Gumball 3000 experience in one word?
Exhilarating and Ageing!

Below: The Lotus is custom fitted with a secret compartment containing chilled champagne and glasses.

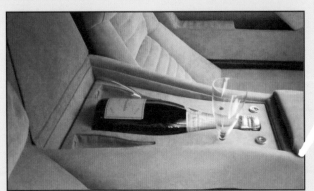

GUMBALL 3000

THE ANNUAL

AN INTRODUCTION

Hello and welcome to the first Gumball 3000 Annual, possibly the next best thing to being on the actual rally itself.

Some of you will know what the Gumball rally is all about. You may have even followed what we've got up to over the past few years on TV and in the thousands of magazine and newspaper articles from around the world? You'll know who some of the regular Gumballers are, and be more than aware of the mischief that goes on for the duration of each years week long, 3000 mile rally.

For those of you that aren't too clued up on what Gumball 3000 is all about, treat this annual as a guide. Whether you're wondering how the event started, where it's visited, or which celebrities from the worlds of film, fashion, music and sport would be mad enough to have entered over the years, you'll find all you need to know, and more right here.

Needless to say the 2003 Gumball rally was a blast, and we here at Gumball HQ are delighted to be able to share the highs and lows with you...and all from the comfort of wherever you're sat reading this. Believe me, the novelty of spending several days in the cramped cockpit of a two seater sports car with the wind in your eyes, your knees up around your ears and an exhausted co-driver sat next to you soon wears off!

You're under starters orders...
On your marks, get set, go!!

Maximillion Cooper.

7

The Story So far...

1999

Maximillion Cooper, founder and organiser of Gumball 3000, had a dream. His ambition was to become a racing driver. At the same time he also had a lot of friends in the worlds of fashion, pop music, media, business...you know the sort. So he decides to throw a party for some of his friends.

Above: McLaren F1 LM eases down the ramp

But it turns out to be not just any old party. Inspired by the cult movie Cannonball Run, this one would see them driving through 6 countries, 2 principalities, visit 5 Grand Prix circuits, covering a total distance of 3000 miles. Not forgetting of course that it had all started as a party, outrageous soirees were planned for every night of the rally, and the fact that they only had 6 days to complete it made it even more challenging. Got that?

Above: 1999 Mercedes CLK GTR prepares for Hockenheim circuit.

They started in London, headed across to Paris, then Monaco via the Le Mans Grand Prix circuit. Rimini in Italy was next, then a visit to the Ferrari factory in Modena. Through The Alps and onto the Hockenheim Grand Prix circuit before heading home to London. Were they mad?

Above: Chris Eubank and his wife Karron with their trophy.

Notable entrants included Dannii Minogue in a Porsche Boxster, and Jason Priestley from Beverly Hills 90210 who swapped autographs for freedom when he was caught driving at 170 mph!

Above Left: Jason Priestley. Above Right: Popstar Dannii Minogue collects her Gumball Tiffany's award.

2000

Apparently they weren't mad, because the following year Max decided to do it all again. Only this time, the word had spread. The great success of the 1999 event had really caught the

Above: Drum 'n' Bass legend Goldie giving the thumb's up in an Aston Martin V8.

imagination of the worlds press, and it seemed that everybody who was anybody had heard all about Max and his crazy jaunts with his mates. He had people banging on his door asking if they could join the rally. Before long the event had grown even bigger, and so had the list of celebrities wanting to join in the fun.

Above Left: Soul Diva Kym Mazelle *Above Right:* Tara P-T

85 cars and 3 motorbikes driving through 7 countries in 6 days. 3000 miles was once again the route distance, and all this didn't seem to put them off. Drum 'n' Bass DJ Goldie and Cass Lewis from Skunk Anansie were in an Aston Martin V8, rock stars Placebo entered in an AM Lagonda, Bez and Nuts from the Happy Mondays were in charge of a top of the range Jaguar, and soul diva Kym Mazelle was chauffeured around the route in a BMW.

Above: 1970 Dodge Challenger with the worlds largest sound system!

Marble Arch in London was the starting line, followed by a short drive to Stansted Airport where the cars were loaded onto 2 Russian Antanov transporter planes. The entrants were loaded on to a private jet, and they met up with their rides upon landing at a private airport in Spain. Bilbao was the first stop, then onto Cannes in the south of France where Max had arranged for a Gumball boat party for the last night of the film festival. Milan was the first port of call for

lunch the following day, before heading to a castle in the middle of Germany's Black Forest.

Above Left: A one off, 1992 Silver Arrow Ferrari F12 LM in traffic!

Next stop was the Nurburgring Grand Prix circuit, then Hamburg to catch a ferry back to England. One last stop at the Lotus Factory, then it was home to London.

2001

The third Gumball rally was a little bit more adventurous. London was the official start again, but they wouldn't be turning around and heading home until they reached Russia!

Above Left: Ferrari 360 on it's way to Helsinki!

After a checkpoint in Berlin, the first stop was Vilnius in Lithuania, which took an average of thirty hours to reach. Next was St Petersburg in Russia for a real 007 party. Helsinki in Finland, Stockholm in Sweden and finally Copenhagen in Denmark before a triumphant arrival back in London. Yet again the Gumball rally had seen an extraordinary 106 cars drive 3000 miles across thirteen countries in just 6 days. Despite the fear of carjacking and lawlessness in eastern Europe, and the fact that Max had employed the services of ex-forces security specialists to help ensure the entrants arrived home in one piece with their cars, it seemed that once again, everybody had a great time.

The Story So Far...

VISKO HATFIELD

Above: Jackass' Chris 'party boy' Pontius as Captain America!

This year the BBC sent Ruby Wax along to film an hour long documentary, and MTV entered Johnny Knoxville, Steve O, and Chris "party boy" Pontius along with the rest of the Jackass team to make an hour long Gumball special.

Above: Comedian Vic Reeves with TV host Ruby Wax

ROSSA COLE

Above: Star-spangled Corvette!

2002

For a change, this year Max and the team decided to try something a little different, and planned a route that would see them driving through just one country. But this time they'd be travelling coast to coast across America, and they'd be passing through 13 States, each with their own immutable law enforcement styles.

JAY CENA

Above: A 2002 Lamborghini Diablo 6.0

A massive line up of 175 cars and 3 motorbikes were on the grid for the start of the 2002 rally in New York. The race then saw them drive the 3000 miles to Los Angeles via Washington DC, Nashville, Elvis' home at Graceland, Dallas, Santa Fe, the Grand Canyon and Las Vegas over the course of the following 6 days.

Above: Hefner and Bunnies welcome Gumballers at the Playboy Mansion

Once again this was quite a challenge - 3000 miles in six days is a tough call for the most experienced of endurance drivers. But as an added incentive, Max had arranged for none other than Mr Hugh Hefner and his Bunnies to meet the exhausted drivers and tend to their every need when they crossed the finish line at the Playboy Mansion. Needless to say most drivers tried their hardest to make it in time.

ROSSA COLE

Above: Team Playboy

2003

America had been such a good host to the Gumball rally in 2002 that Max decided to take the event back again, only this time they'd be driving across the other way. The big difference this year was that the mixed bag of Gumballers would be joined by a film crew that included helicopters and over a hundred cameras who would be filming throughout the event to make Gumball 3000 'The Movie'.

Above: F50 leads the way

Now like a lot of people, some celebrities really can't help themselves when they know there's a camera being pointed at them. Skateboard God Tony Hawk drove a new Dodge Viper, the Jackass guys rented a Cadillac, and the Cuban Brothers ended up break dancing naked at each party. Freestyle Motor X champion Carey Hart jumped a line of cars in Las Vegas, and the others, well I guess you'll just have to watch the movie to find out what they got up to.

Above: Skateboard legend Tony Hawk

San Francisco Mayor Willie Brown took time out from his busy schedule to lead a procession of the 150 cars that entered this year's event around the city before waving the start flag from the Ferrari F50 he was being carried in. Reno was the first stop, then onto Tucson before spinning doughnuts in the sand at the White Sands missile

Above: The Mayor of San Francisco, Willie Brown

base in New Mexico. San Antonio and New Orleans were the final two stages before heading towards the finish line in Miami. Another 3000 miles covered, another unforgettable memory for everybody that entered. Oh, and a feature film for everyone else to watch as well - not bad for 6 days work.

Above: The Koenigsegg CC - the world fastest car

2004

Visit www.gumball3000.com for all the details of the Gumball rally in 2004...

To Be Continued..

Welcome
...To San Fransisco

The Mayor of San Francisco welcomes Gumballers and Gumball fans to his beautiful city...

Above: Mayor Willie Brown

BO BRIDGES

ON THE GRID

It's just hours before the start of the rally...
The adrenaline is beginning to flow in earnest,
and not just for the competitors....

Above: The Mayor of San Francisco

Above: The Koenigsegg CC - a final check!

Above: I spy a RUF Porsche!

Above: Porsche – quietly confident!

Above: Steve Crompton's BMW E46 M3 Convertible

SAN FRAN

Above: Lining up on California Street

Above: Scrutinizing!

Above: The Koenigsegg CC under scrutiny!

Above: The Cadillac getting stickered up!

Above: Ferrari, Lambo, Ferrari! Below: F50 ready for take off!

Above: Ah! A little Lotus!

AND THEY'RE OFF!!

BRIAN BIRD

Above: Gentleman, start your engines!

NICK THOMSON

Go!

NICK THOMSON

Go!!

Go!!!

JIM STONEBURNER

Above: A Lambo, Ferrari and Jaguar follow a BMW down Lombard Stree

Above: Watch out, there's a Prowler on the loose!

Above: Max's Murcielago heads for Reno

Above: Ever seen one of these before?

Above: Karta's potato fuelled Kenworth truck leaves San Francisco!

BIRDMAN!

BO BRIDGES

Q&A:

What is your ultimate Gumball car?
Ferrari Modena

What's your daily ride?
Lexus LS430

What's your favourite car related movie?
Smokey and the Bandit

What's your favourite music?
The Clash, Jane's Addiction, Coldplay, Radiohead, Dr Dre

What's your favourite clothing brand?
Quiksilver

What's your favourite magazine?
Colors

Who is your greatest hero of all time?
My Dad

What's the most outrageous thing you've ever done?
Had kids (3 crazy boys)

What was your worst moment on the Gumball?
Getting pulled over just outside of Reno

What was your best moment on the Gumball?
Hitting 160 mph in the Viper on the way to Vegas

Who from history would be your dream Gumball co-driver?
Steve McQueen or James Dean

Sum up your Gumball 3000 experience in one word?
Rush...

What do you write about the man who inspired a major part of your own youth and is still running the skate arena today when your own board was hung up a long time ago?

Given his first skateboard at the age of 9 by his brother, Tony quickly changed from nightmare adolescent into the model skater. Sponsored at 12, professional by the time he was 14, and by the time he'd reached 16 he was the best skater in the world!

Now proud founder of skate company Birdhouse Projects, star of his fifth international best-selling computer game, organiser of the annual Boom Boom Huckjam tour and father of 3 boys, it's amazing how he still finds the time to skate at all?

Tony Hawk

ATIBA JEFFERSON

GUMBALLER PROFILE:

Name:

TONY HAWK

Age: 35

Nationality: USA

Home Town: San Diego

Occupation: Professional Skateboarder

Career highlights: Winning a few competitions and having a signature video game

Make of car driven in the Gumball: 2003 Dodge Viper

Above: The legend Birdman in full flight and fully committed.

BO BRIDGES

"DUDE, WHERES MY CAR?"

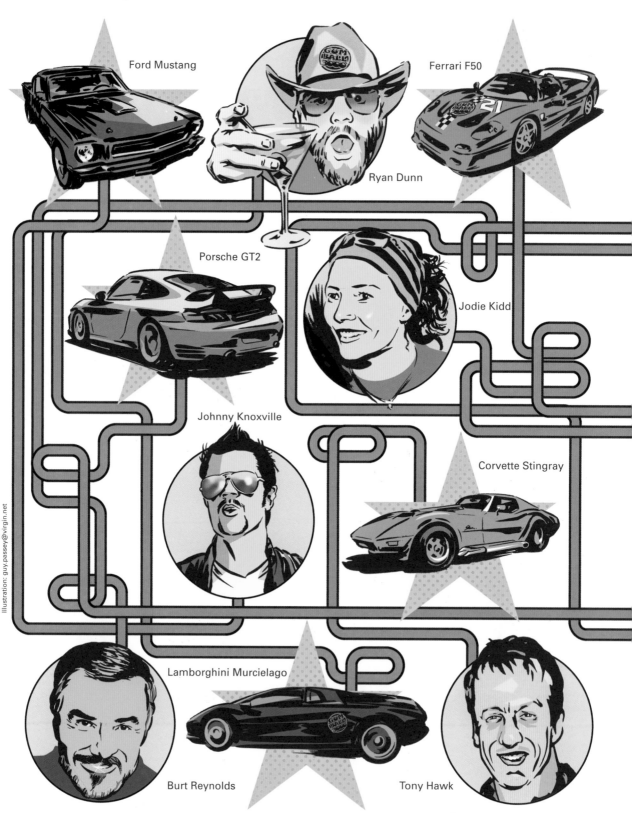

Ford Mustang

Ryan Dunn

Ferrari F50

Porsche GT2

Jodie Kidd

Johnny Knoxville

Corvette Stingray

Lamborghini Murcielago

Burt Reynolds

Tony Hawk

Illustration: guy.passey@virgin.net

Torino, Tony Hawk – Corvette Stingray, Maximillion Cooper – BMW M5 'Polizei', Har Mar Superstar – Porsche GT2, Cuban Bros – Koenigsegg, Shane Slevin – Ferrari F50

After a wild party our gumballers have over slept. In the rush to get back on track, they grab the first keys they can find. Can you help them find their cars?!?!

Ford Torino

Maximillion Cooper

Har Mar Superstar

Cadillac Deville

The Cuban Bros

Koenigsegg

BMW M5 'Polizei'

Shane Slevin

OUTLAW JESSE JAMES!

BO BRIDGES

Founder and owner of West Coast Choppers, as well as presenter on Discovery Channel's Monster Garage, Jesse has come a long way since his days as a professional bodyguard for the likes of Slayer, Danzig and Soundgarden to name but a few.

Before that it was football, but it would appear that Jesse has discovered his vocation, and is often found getting his hands dirty doing what he loves best - customising motorbikes, cars, trucks...and pretty much anything else with wheels and an engine!

BO BRIDGES

THE CAR IS THE STAR!!!

VW EUROVAN - 'YOOHOO' VAN

Max speed (mph):	115
0-60 (seconds):	11.2
Max power (bhp):	201
Miles per gallon (mpg):	17
Engine capacity (cc):	2800
Cost when new:	$33,640
Total produced:	n/a
Gumball Factor:	70%

"Flamed, lowered, have you ever seen a camper like it!"

Above: 'Nasty' firecrackers Arizona!

NICK THOMSON

Above: Jesse with wife Jannie on the starting grid.

Q&A:

What is your ultimate Gumball car?
1930 Stutz Buffoon
What's your daily ride?
1954 Chevy
What's your favourite car related movie?
The Car of Doom
What's your favourite music?
Slayer
What's your favourite clothing brand?
West Coast Choppers
What's your favourite magazine?
Aeroplane
Who is your greatest hero of all time?
Don Potts
What's the most outrageous thing you've ever done?
Sorry. Heavily censored!!!
What was your worst moment on the Gumball?
Getting arrested in Reno
What was your best moment on the Gumball?
Getting out of jail in Reno
Who from history would be your dream Gumball co-driver?
Satan
Sum up your Gumball 3000 experience in one word?
Lame!!

★ Custom Flame Paint
★ Lowered
★ 20% Jesse James Style 44 Triple Plated Chrome Wheels
★ Kicker Stereo
★ GameBoy Advance SP Games

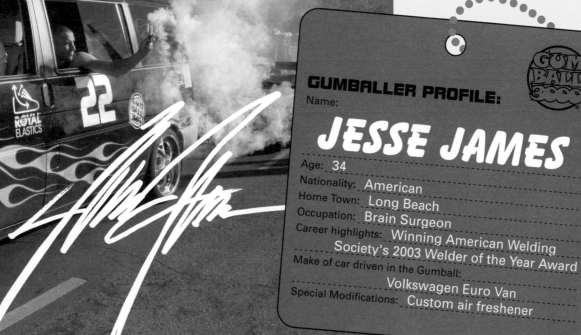

GUMBALLER PROFILE:
Name:

JESSE JAMES

Age: 34
Nationality: American
Home Town: Long Beach
Occupation: Brain Surgeon
Career highlights: Winning American Welding Society's 2003 Welder of the Year Award
Make of car driven in the Gumball: Volkswagen Euro Van
Special Modifications: Custom air freshener

Q&A:

What is your ultimate Gumball car?
A pink Ferrari

What's your everyday ride?
1963 Impala convertible

What's your favourite car related movie?
Gone in 60 seconds

What's your favourite music?
Anything hip hop at the moment

What's your favourite clothing brand?
Hurley

What's your favourite magazine?
Any snowboarding mag that has pictures of my friends in it

Who is your greatest hero of all time?
I looked up to Nadia Comaneci when she won the gold medal with a perfect 10 in gymnastics

What's the most outrageous thing you've ever done?
Trying to get a mini van to do over 100 mph at 4am in the middle of the desert

What was your worst moment on the Gumball?
Stopping for gas at 3am and then driving into the desert for 30 miles before we realised that none of the five members of our team had put gas in the tank. We had to turn around and go back to fill up as the next gas station wasn't for another 60 miles

What was your best moment on the Gumball?
Arriving in Reno to a huge crowd of people all cheering for us! It was the best

Who from history would be your dream Gumball co-driver?
Burt Reynolds

Sum up your Gumball 3000 experience in one word?
Fast!

GUMBALLER PROFILE:

Name: **TINA BASICH**

Age: 34

Nationality: American

Home Town: Sacramento, California

Occupation: Professional Snowboarder

Career highlights: Co-founder of Boarding for Breast Cancer, Gold medal X Games Big Air 1998, 2nd place World Championships Big Air 2000

Make of car driven in the Gumball: 2003 Volkswagen Euro Van

Special Modifications: Jesse James went to town on it. New rims, lowered, with a fire paint job. The engine was also modified.

LAS VEGAS

checkpoint

It would be fair to say that Tina's been snowboarding for a while. A long while in fact. She was offered her first sponsorship deal way back in 1988, and has been pushing the limits of her sport and winning competitions ever since, placing her very firmly within the elite of the snowboarding community. Tina's 2003 Gumball rally experience must have been fantastic. Just read for yourself...

Tara Dakides started skiing when she was 13, but quickly discovered the joys of riding sideways and fell into skateboarding. As it is for many others, snowboarding seemed like a logical step, and she's now riding high amongst the worlds best. World renowned for her innovative and ballsy riding style, as well as her blessed good looks, Tara really is pretty damn good...for a girl!!

Q&A:

What is your ultimate Gumball car?
A pink Ferrari Testarossa
What's your daily ride?
Chevy diesel truck
What's your favourite car related movie?
Smokey and the Bandit
What's your favourite music?
Music I can dance to...beats
What's your favourite clothing brand?
I love too many to have one favourite
What's your favourite magazine?
Nylon and I.D.
Who is your greatest hero of all time?
Superman
What's the most outrageous thing you've ever done?
I can't disclose that information
What was your worst moment on the Gumball?
Leaving
What was your best moment on the Gumball?
The rest of the time
Who from history would be your dream Gumball co-driver?
Brad Pitt
Sum up your Gumball 3000 experience in one word?
Adventurous

GUMBALLER PROFILE:

Name:
TARA DAKIDES

Age: 28
Nationality: American
Home Town: Mission Viejo, California
Occupation: Professional Snowboarder
Career highlights: Winning numerous competitions and gold medals
Make of car driven in the Gumball:
2003 Volkswagen Euro Van

Above: Bo Bridges at the wheel of the Volkswagen on the Las Vegas Bullring Speedway

The end of the first day, with 677 miles completed, brings the drivers to downtown Las Vegas and the Mandalay Bay Hotel...

Image sequence taken from Gumball 3000 'The Movie'!

28

GUMBALLER PROFILE:

Name:

CAREY HART

Age: 29

Nationality: American

Home Town: Las Vegas

Occupation: Professional Freestyle Moto X rider

Career highlights: Far too many competition placings and wins to mention

Make of car driven in the Gumball: Mercedes Benz CL 500

Special Modifications: Hart attack! (Carey's signature trick)

MIKE SHARTIS

MIKE SHARTIS

checkpoint

LAS VEGAS

THE FAMILIE

CELEBRITY CARS
LAS VEGAS

HART ATTACK!

Carey Hart's name and style are as synonymous with Moto X as Matt Hoffman is to BMX or Steve Caballero is to skateboarding. He was given his first bike at the age of 4, and spent the majority of his formative years dominating the Supercross circuit. It was shortly after leaving High School that he discovered Moto X, and the rest, as they say, is history. With a string of competition wins and placings, hordes of magazine interviews and film and chat show appearances, as well as the accolade of being the first rider to ever pull a backflip on a 250cc motorcycle, you can be left in no doubt that Carey Hart has well and truly earned his place in the Moto X Hall of Fame.

Q&A:

What is your ultimate Gumball car?
Mercedes SL 500 convertible

What's your daily ride?
Mitsubishi factory race Lancer rally car

What's your favourite car related movie?
Days of Thunder

What's your favourite music?
Punk, metal, hip hop

What's your favourite clothing brand?
Hurley

What's your favourite magazine?
Tattoo magazine

Who is your greatest hero of all time?
My Dad

What's the most outrageous thing you've ever done?
I wouldn't even know where to start. Look at my job!

What was your worst moment on the Gumball?
Getting a 135 mph ticket in a 55

What was your best moment on the Gumball?
I was only in it for one day, but probably starting almost dead last and working my way up to top 5 before getting pulled over

Who from history would be your dream Gumball co-driver?
Jim Morrison. What a trip

Sum up your Gumball 3000 experience in one word?
Expensive

BO BRIDGES

Q&A:

What is your ultimate Gumball car?
BMW 7 series

What's your daily ride?
2003 Ford F250 diesel

What's your favourite car related movie?
Cannonball Run

What's your favourite music?
Punk

What's your favourite clothing brand?
Billabong

What's your favourite magazine?
Transworld MX

Who is your greatest hero of all time?
My Parents

What's the most outrageous thing you've ever done?
Everyday is more outrageous than the one before

What was your worst moment on the Gumball?
Not being able to race

What was your best moment on the Gumball?
Jumping for all the participants

Who from history would be your dream Gumball co-driver?
Burt Reynolds

Sum up your Gumball 3000 experience in one word?
VEGAS

> "People ask me do you have any time for hobbies? I'm fortunate enough to be able to say to them that my whole life is one big hobby. I get to go all over and do what I want. It can be hard work, but I love it."
> JEFF TILTON

MIKE SHARTIS

MIKE SHARTIS

GUMBALLER PROFILE:

Name: **JEFF TILTON**

Age: 27
Nationality: American
Home Town: Temecula, CA
Occupation: Pro moto X rider
Career highlights: Winner of three Vans Triple Crown whip contests, 5th X games step up, Winner Bluetorch Survivor series

Above: Jeff meets the Cuban Brothers.

Q&A:

What is your ultimate Gumball car?
Bentley

What's your daily ride?
Supercrew F-50

What's your favourite music?
Punk Rock

What's your favourite clothing brand?
Globe

What's your favourite magazine?
Playboy, Hustler, anything with chicks

Who is your greatest hero of all time?
Myself

What's the most outrageous thing you've ever done?
To many to name

What was your worst moment on the Gumball?
Being too hungover to ride

What was your best moment on the Gumball?
Anytime when all the chicks were around.

Who from history would be your dream Gumball co-driver?
My chick

Sum up your Gumball 3000 experience in one word?
Sick

"I just love riding bikes hard cause the girls just love it when I do it hard"
JUDD WILLIAMS

MIKE SHARTIS

MIKE SHARTIS

GUMBALLER PROFILE:

Name:

JUDD WILLIAMS

Age: 25
Nationality: American
Home Town: Vegas
Occupation: Sales Manager, Freestyle rider, custom steel furniture fabricator
Career highlights: Warp tour and many other demos

MIKE SHARTIS

Above: Judd, Jeff and Carey prepare for action!

SEEING RED!

★★★★★★★★★★★★

The 2003 Gumball Rally saw the most incredible array of Supercars take part. Amongst the forty or so Ferrari's, one stood out more than the rest – The F50 Spider.

The Ferrari F50 was designed to commemorate Ferrari's 50th anniversary in 1996. Only 349 F50s were made in Ferrari's factory near Modeno in northern Italy, purposely one less than the predicted market for this limited edition model so that they would be hard to find. The F50 was the first and last car Ferrari were able to build based on a Formula 1 engine due to the imminent tougher global emission standards that were about to come into effect.

Half the cars had been reserved before the car was even available! Fifty each were sold in the United States, Germany and Italy, Ferrari's biggest markets. Most of the others were sold in Asia and elsewhere in Europe. It's rumoured that Mike Tyson was the first American to get his hands on an F50 at a cost of $850,000!

MIKE SHARTIS

THE CAR IS THE STAR!!!

1996 FERRARI F50 SPIDER	
Max speed (mph):	202
0-60 (seconds):	3.7
Max power (bhp):	520
Miles per gallon (mpg):	8
Engine capacity (cc):	4699
Cost when new:	$480,000
Total produced:	349
Gumball Factor:	98%

"A wolf in wolf's clothing!"

ANTONIO ALVENDIA, www.ciphergarage.com

Above: The F50 was one of the many supercars on display at the LA premiere of Gumball 3000 'The Movie'.

MIKE SHARTIS

Above: Charles Morgan puts his Aero 8 through its paces.

MIKE SHARTIS

Above: Ferrari F50 launches up the straight!

checkpoint

PHOENIX

Above: Porsche GT2 pedal to the metal!

Above: Fly at the wheel of the Subaru WRX!

Welcome to Firebird International Raceway, where Gumballers got a legal chance to put pedal to the metal and really put their cars through their paces! The 1.6 mile road race course utilises a 1/4 mile 'dragstrip' with 14 turns and a 5/8 mile straight away (who said America has no bends!). The Ferrari F50 won all straight-line battles, and after a few laps of laying down rubber it was back on the road to Tucson....

Main image: Catch me if you can!! A 360 Modena, an F50 and two Porsche Carrera's follow the VW Euro Van up the drag strip!

Gumball Girls

Every year the Gumball seems to attract a whole bunch of female drivers… they come in all shapes and sizes and get into all sorts of trouble!

EYHAB JUMEAN

Above: Lady V gets off on the speeding fine!

Above: Playmate Miss July (1997), Daphnee Duplaix puts her mini through its paces!

Above: Playmate Miss December (2001), Shanna Moakler gets off lightly!

Above: Even nurse Cynthia got into a little trouble!

Above: And 'Sue' was a real handful!

Cop: We don't condone driving like that here in Snatchville County young lady, but I'm prepared to turn a blind eye today"

Gumball Swedish Babe: "Thank you so much officer, I promise I'll be more careful next time" (she said whilst clutching her beaver)

JACK POLLICK

F-U
♡ Johnny Knoxville

GUMBALLER PROFILE:

Name:

JOHNNY KNOXVILLE

Age: 32
Nationality: American
Home Town: South Knoxville, Tenessee
Occupation: Former basic cable star
Career highlights: Still waiting
Make of car driven in the Gumball:
1989 Beater Jaguar
Special Modifications: No way! We only got it 10 minutes before the start!

VISKO HATFIELD

HELLO, I'M
JOHNNY KNOXVILLE

Main image: Johnny at home with his friends. Below left: Max and Johnny discuss tactics! Below right: Pontius, Johnny and Steve O polish their Jag.

Born Philip John Clapp, the son of a car salesman, Johnny was raised in Knoxville, Tennessee. His big break came after shooting himself with pepper spray, a taser, a stun gun, and .38 magnum as part of a feature on 'self-defence' whilst working for Big Brother skateboarding magazine.

Johnny quickly became a cult hero and soon there was a bidding war between MTV and Comedy Central to land him a TV show. He was offered a spot on Saturday Night Live, but turned it down. That's when Johnny Knoxville, Jeff Tremaine, and Spike Jonze pitched the idea of Jackass to MTV. Jackass quickly became one of the cable's highest rated shows and eventually sparked many recent movie deals for Johnny including a big screen version of Jackass, Men in Black II, and Grand Theft Parsons. Most recently he has starred in the Farrelly brothers latest film, 'The Ringer', where he pretends he is disabled in order to compete in the Special Olympics. The movie is expected to be released next year.

Johnny's participation in the Gumball was immortalised after he took part in the 2001 rally, from London to Russia, which was turned into an hour long Jackass Gumball 3000 Special on MTV. The show received MTV's highest ratings of the year!

Q&A:

What is your ultimate Gumball car?
Next time I'm taking a tour bus full of athletically built young men

What's your daily ride?
1970 Cadillac Eldorado

What's your favourite car related movie?
Smokey and the Bandit 3

What's your favourite music?
Negro Spirituals

What's your favourite clothing brand?
Anything with a breathable pantsuit

What's your favourite magazine?
American Grizzly

Who is your greatest hero of all time?
Shane Slevin

What's the most outrageous thing you've ever done?
Watching Steve O and Partyboy loon around in the car as we drove through London

What was your worst moment on the Gumball?
The first 60 hours of the Russian Gumball during which I only slept for 2!

What was your best moment on the Gumball?
The car's never been the same since!

Who from history would be your dream Gumball co-driver?
Abdullah the Butcher

Sum up your Gumball 3000 experience in one word?
Totally fked!**

ON THE ROAD

For Gumballers the open road is a place to relax, sit back, take in the scenery, and floor it!!!!

Main image: A Ferrari F50 at speed!!

BO BRIDGES

Oregon
GUMBAL

MIKE SHARTIS

Above: Bullitt!

Above: Yorgo a go go!

Above: I'm Dunn!

Above: Rent a car, put a number on it

Above: 'Vette waiting for action!

Above: BMW Z8 flyin by!

Above: Lotus Elise on US ashpalt!

EVEN SUPERMODELS DO THE GUMBALL!

The daughter of polo legend Johnny Kidd, Jodie Kidd is probably best known for her regular appearances on the world's catwalks and on the covers of international fashion magazines. But these days you're more likely to find her on the polo field, enthusiastically following in the footsteps of both her father and her brother Jack. This darling of the fashion world is currently taking the rich kids game by storm, and having a whale of a time doing it. Recent photo shoots have depicted her in many guises on horseback, and it seems all the world's media want to discuss with her during interviews is polo. Business and pleasure, the hardest yet most satisfying reward.

THE CAR IS THE STAR!!!

2003 DODGE VIPER

Max speed (mph):	117
0-60 (seconds):	4.6
Max power (bhp):	381
Miles per gallon (mpg):	14.1
Engine capacity (cc):	7990
Cost when new:	$68,825
Total produced:	n/a
Gumball Factor:	65%

"An all American brute!"

BRIAN BIRD

Q&A:

What is your ultimate Gumball car?
Maserati or Bentley GT
What's your daily ride?
Maserati Spyder
What's your favourite car related movie?
The original Italian Job
What's your favourite music?
Trance
What's your favourite clothing brand?
Diesel and Missoni
What's your favourite magazine?
Dazed & Confused
Who is your greatest hero of all time?
My Dad
What's the most outrageous thing you've ever done?
Not telling
What was your worst moment on the Gumball?
My Hermes Birkin bag getting run over by an 18 wheeler on the Florida turnpike
What was your best moment on the Gumball?
Driving
Who from history would be your dream Gumball co-driver?
Bob Marley
Sum up your Gumball 3000 experience in one word?
Vavavoom...

GUMBALLER PROFILE:

Name:

JODIE KIDD

Age: 25
Nationality: British
Home Town: Ifold, Sussex
Occupation: Model
Career highlights: Read a newspaper
Make of car driven in the Gumball:
2003 Dodge Viper Convertible

BRITISH BATMOBILE!

With it's hi-tech ZZ Top hot-rod attitude and graceful 1930's styling, a wolf in sheep's clothing would be an appropriate way to describe the popular Aero 8, proving once and for all that Morgan are a force to be reckoned with. This is the first completely new Morgan for 60 years, and like it or not, there's no denying that a lot of thought has gone into the way this car looks. But it's the BMW V8 under the bonnet and the handling of this superb car that really does do the British manufacturer proud.

Everybody knows that the only way to drive a Morgan is with the hood down and the wind in your ears, but with a top speed of 160 mph on the track you'd better hold onto your hat!!

★ The first new Morgan in over 30 years earned it's stripes under the right foot of Charles Morgan on four consecutive rallies.

"I love cars and travel and the Gumball gives me an opportunity to indulge in both. Driving has always been a passion and I have used the Gumball to try out cars and technical products and see if they can be improved. With the lightweight Morgan Aero 8 GTN I reckon you have just about the ultimate Gumball car, fast, nimble, economical and comfortable, without being a luxury cruiser. It's as near as you can get at the moment to a practical racing car for the road. That's not to say that its perfect and I will need to do a lot more Gumballs to continue on my search for perfection." CHARLES MORGAN

THE CAR IS THE STAR!!!

2002 MORGAN AERO 8

Max speed (mph):	160
0-60 (seconds):	4.9
Max power (bhp):	286
Miles per gallon (mpg):	26
Engine capacity (cc):	4398
Cost when new:	$81,000
Total produced:	250
Gumball Factor:	82%

"Part 'Batmobile', part ballistic missile!"

Above: The Aero 8 turned heads more than most, with spectators in awe of it's unique looks!

Above: Charles poses with his flagship motor!

Q&A:

What is your ultimate Gumball car?
Morgan Aero 8 GTN

What's your daily ride?
Morgan Aero 8 GTN

What's your favourite car related movie?
Two Lane Blacktop

What's your favourite music?
Vivaldi's Four Seasons

What's your favourite clothing brand?
Richard James

What's your favourite magazine?
Intersection

Who is your greatest hero of all time?
HFS Morgan, my Grandfather

What's the most outrageous thing you've ever done?
Walking into Afghanistan - the Mujhadeen behind Russian lines

What was your worst moment on the Gumball?
Nearly arrested in Alabama for relieving myself in the bushes

What was your best moment on the Gumball?
Finishing 3rd in Miami in 2003

Who from history would be your dream Gumball co-driver?
My wife, Kira

Sum up your Gumball 3000 experience in one word?
Addictive

GUMBALLER PROFILE:

Name:

CHARLES MORGAN

Age: 53

Nationality: British

Home Town: Malvern

Occupation: Managing Director

Career highlights: Morgan Aero 8 Launch, Geneva Show 2004, Winning a Silver Nymph, Monte Carlo TV Festival 1981, Winning the BRDC Production Sports Car Championship, 1978

Make of car driven in the Gumball: Morgan Aero 8

WHITE SANDS MISSILE RANGE

BIRTHPLACE OF AMERICA'S MISSILE & SPACE ACTIVITY

DAN MERMELSTEIN

Burt Reynolds; "Today's checkpoint was the unusual setting of White Sands Missile Base."

Gumballers ate hot dogs and doughnuts at White Sands Missile Range in New Mexico on the way to The Alamo in San Antonio. White Sands is the busiest US missile range, its full of big b***ard missiles.

When people visit the United States, a lot of people don't visit places like this, I don't blame them." MIGUEL MONTEVANI

DOUGHNUTS FOR LUNCH?

MIKE SHARTIS

YORGO TLOUPAS

BO BRIDGES

Above: Our beautiful Lambo girl shows off the missiles!

YORGO TLOUPAS

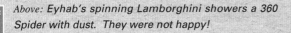

Above: Eyhab's spinning Lamborghini showers a 360 Spider with dust. They were not happy!

MIKE SHARTIS

Q&A:

What is your ultimate Gumball car?
A tour bus with an Enzo as a lead car

What's your everyday ride?
2003 BMW M3 SMG

What's your favourite car related movie?
Smokey and the Bandit

What's your favourite music?
Bad Brains, Beatnuts, Radiohead

What's your favourite clothing brand?
Billabong

What's your favourite magazine?
Racer

Who is your greatest hero of all time?
Spiderman

What's the most outrageous thing you've ever done?
Drank all night and did an early TV morning show at the crack of dawn with no sleep, then knocked myself out on live TV

What was your worst moment on the Gumball?
Waking up with a hangover every morning

What was your best moment on the Gumball?
Going all out the whole way with my co-pilots and all ending with no tickets

Who from history would be your dream Gumball co-driver?
The same one I always have. The man himself, Jesus Christ

Sum up your Gumball 3000 experience in one word?
Comradery

GUMBALLER PROFILE:

Name: BUCKY LASEK

Age: 30
Nationality: American
Home Town: Baltimore, Md
Occupation: Skateboarder
Career highlights: "Too many to list, ...and that's a great thing"
Make of car driven in the Gumball: 2004 Type SR Jaguar

BO BRIDGES

Bucky Lasek has been skating for seventeen years. He rides Vert (that's the big ramp for the uninitiated) and to put it simply, he's very good. So good in fact that you'd be hard pushed to not find a picture or a mention of his name in any skateboarding magazine you might decide to pick up and read.

He has a list of sponsors and credits that many a fellow skater would quite happily give any limb for, and an army of fans that worship his innovative style. Ladies and gentleman, allow me to present Bucky Lasek

Main image: After taking part in the Gumball, 2003 was an amazing year for Bucky, winning Gold medals at the Gravity Games, X-Games and Vans Triple Crown. Unreal!

Bucky Lasek
Jarod DeAnda
Victor Carrillo

DAN MERMELSTEIN

BUCKY WINS GOLD!

BO BRIDGES

ALEX ROY

Above: 2004, Jaguar Type SR

BO BRIDGES

Above: Bucky rocks a Gumball sticker on his deck!

THAT ISN'T A CAR, IT'S A FIGHTER PLANE!

"Not bad for a project spearheaded by a 29 year old and designed by a 20 something year old Aussie!!!!" is just one of the many quotes heard from fans of the Koenigsegg CC.

The independent car manufacturer's project was funded by the Swedish government, and has gone down a storm amongst super car fans around the world. "This is for sure the most beautiful car I've ever seen", "Never thought the Swedes were capable of making cars this cool!!!" and "This car is even more beautiful in real life than it is on pictures" are just some of the more common exclamations heard when people see it – it would appear that praise for this exceptionally rare car knows no bounds. One computer games manufacturer was so impressed by the Koenigsegg and it's 242 mph antics on the Gumball rally that they made it the ultimate car on the hardest and final level of one of their games!!

★ Sweden's first supercar is officially the fastest street-legal production car available!

THE CAR IS THE STAR!!!

CHEW.TV

2003 KOENIGSEGG CC	
Max speed (mph):	240
0-60 (seconds):	3.5
Max power (bhp):	650
Miles per gallon (mpg):	14
Engine capacity (cc):	4710
Cost when new:	$425,000
Total produced:	7
Gumball Factor:	95%

"Could this be the car to take Mclaren's mantle?"

Above: Now that's a supercar!

Above: Inside the fighter plane!

TRAVIS 'CORKSCREW' PASTRANA!

VICTOR CARILLO

Above: Don't try this at home kids!

Travis Pastrana has something of a reputation amongst a certain element of the Motor X crowd. He's often accused of not dedicating himself enough to his sport, and he could be doing better if only he applied himself a little more.

One of the main reasons these comments are directed at him is because he occasionally takes time out from his hectic racing schedule to do things like the Gumball rally. You know, fun things that can provide that all too often overlooked break from the ordinary.

His list of competition wins and bulging trophy cabinet speak volumes. This boy just wants to have fun.

Q&A:

What is your ultimate Gumball car?
Ferrari F40 or a Cadillac convertible with a NASCAR engine

What's your daily ride?
Either an F-350 or a 1944 International

What's your favourite car related movie?
Gone in 60 seconds

What's your favourite music?
Lincoln Park or Chuck Berry

What's your favourite clothing brand?
Puma

What's your favourite magazine?
Racer X or Maxim

Who is your greatest hero of all time?
Matt Hoffman

What's the most outrageous thing you've ever done?
Launched my Suzuki off the Grand Canyon, pulled a back flip then let go and pulled a parachute

GUMBALLER PROFILE:

Name:

TRAVIS PASTRANA

Age: 19

Nationality: American

Home Town: Annapolis, Maryland

Occupation: Pro Motorcycle Racer

Career highlights: 4 X-Games gold medals
6 times AMA National Champion
5 Gravity Games Gold medals

Make of car driven in the Gumball: 2000 Porsche 911-
Turbo. Off the showroom floor in Vegas

What was your worst moment on the Gumball?
Getting my first three tickets in less than 5 miles in some podunk town in Arizona. The first one I deserved, but the next two they slapped me with racing and reckless endangerment when I was getting passed by everyone else while I was doing the speed limit in the slow lane!

What was your best moment on the Gumball?
We were in the front of a pack of 4 other silver Porsche 911's doing about 170mph when a cop came the other way on the freeway. We immediately exited and the others kept running. After filling up with fuel, we returned to the highway and two of the others were being handcuffed on the side of the road with the biggest smiles on their faces. Of course we honked and waved as we went by and our fellow jailbait Gumballers just about got sacked when they tried to wave back. Why that was a good experience... I don't know, but man what a rush!

Who from history would be your dream Gumball co-driver?
Bill Clinton or Dolly Parton

Sum up your Gumball 3000 experience in one word?
Tickets

IT'S NOT A RACE IT'S A RALLY!

★★★★★★★★★★★★★★

Adored by Porsche purists and despised by Sunday drivers, its proud owners hold the Porsche 911 GT2 in very high esteem. Lucky drivers, admiring fans and the slow people it's overtaking are left open mouthed in its wake the world over.

Thirty years of development at Porsche's German Development Centre in Weissach has obviously been well spent. Not surprisingly, the decades of fine tuning and sports car engineering seem to have paid off, and judging from all the positive response, the 911 GT2 is the nearest they've come to perfection.

Encapsulating the very best of Porsche's track racing experience, both on and off the tarmac, this car is a remarkable example of how Porsche motor sport experience and technology can be adapted for the road. The quickest and most powerful 911 to date, the GT2 is one hell of a ride. We like.

MIKE SHARTIS

THE CAR IS THE STAR!!!

PORSCHE 911 GT2

Max speed (mph):	198
0-60 (seconds):	4
Max power (bhp):	456
Miles per gallon (mpg):	22
Engine capacity (cc):	3600
Cost when new:	$192,000
Total produced:	n/a
Gumball Factor:	71%

"When a regular 911 just isn't enough!!"

MIKE SHARTIS

Above: Porsche GT2; in pole position!

"It's silver, it's modified and it's f**king hauling ass!!"

Above: Porsche GT2; No messin!

checkpoint

HOUSTON

Q&A:

What is your ultimate Gumball car?

Two lazy boys and an engine

What's your daily ride?

Escalade

What's your favourite car related movie?

Stroker Ace

What's your favourite music?

Anything you can't dance to

What's your favourite clothing brand?

Little devil

What's your favourite magazine?

FHM

Who is your greatest hero of all time?

The greatest American hero

What's the most outrageous thing you've ever done?

They can't show it here!

What was your worst moment on the Gumball?

Dimitry playing the Mammas and the Pappas for 6 hours straight

What was your best moment on the Gumball?

Dimitry driving down the wrong side of the road, singing People who need people

Who from history would be your dream Gumball co-driver?

Johnny Cash

Sum up your Gumball 3000 experience in one word?

Supercalafragalisticespialido uchous (I just wanted to see if I could spell that)

Ryan Dunn, anti-hero of MTV's Jackass and CKY skate videos. Along with the rest of the crew, this man has inflicted excruciating amounts of pain, fear and humiliation upon himself, and all in the name of entertainment.

With several series of the now cult TV programme, a assortment of movie appearances and the infamous CKY empire under his belt, you have to wonder what drives such a person to potentially harm himself in so many different ways, so often?

A full colour poster of Ryan is available to buy from our website shop at: www.gumball3000.com

Ryan: "It's basically like watching 'Cannonball Run''. They're just in it for the fun. Nobody's trying to get to the finish line. There isn't even a finish line. It's just a party every night and it's the fun of getting in trouble on the way to a party every night for five days straight. It's unbelievable to see just the chaos going on."

GUMBALLER PROFILE:

Name:

RYAN DUNN

Age: 26

Nationality: American

Home Town: West Chester, Pennsylvania

Occupation: Random moron

Career highlights: Meeting Iggy Pop

Make of car driven in the Gumball: 2002 Cadillac Deville Rental Car

JOE WINDSOR WILLIAMS

MIKE SHARTIS

BO BRIDGES

Above: Dunn and co-pilot Jackass comrade Dimitry prepare to test America's biggest fireworks!

Above: The expression of a man with a car up his bum!

59

EYHAB JUMEAN

EYHAB JUMEAN

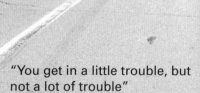

Most cars are on their way to the next check-point. Some aren't so lucky.

BO BRIDGES

NICK THOMSON

Vicky brought her Lamborghini over from England to give it a taste of the spirit of the Gumball. But she discovered that the game of cat and mouse between Gumballers and cops can be a costly one.

"You get in a little trouble, but not a lot of trouble"

BO BRIDGES

"WITHOUT THE COPS I DON'T THINK IT'D BE THAT INTERESTING. THEY'RE WHAT MAKE IT CHALLENGING."

"I'm going to issue you with a citation...." (part of the Gumball initiation procedure)

"Its uncle time, its nephew time, its nice to touch. Lets go."

The Cuban Brothers unusual brand of entertainment is nothing if not individual. Notoriously outrageous, their combined talents of singing, dancing and comedy are skilfully mixed to entertain the most difficult of crowds at the most nerve racking of parties. Miguel and Archerio who used to make regular appearances at Manumission in Ibiza are currently entertainers of choice, making regular appearances at many a celebrity birthday party and magazine award ceremony, as well as being regular guests on MTV!

Shyness is obviously an affliction that these two have never had to deal with, more often than not seen wearing the skimpiest of swimming trunks, if not totally naked whilst breakdancing in front of a crowd. Not a pretty sight.

Q&A - MIGUEL:

What is your ultimate Gumball car?
1957 Chevrolet Drop Head

What's your daily ride?
1959 Mercedes 300SL

What's your favourite car related movie?
Smokey and the Bandit

What's your favourite music?
Salsa, soul, son-son hip hop

What's your favourite clothing brand?
55 DSL adapted by my personal outfitter, Brian Buftamante

What's your favourite magazine?
Dazed & Confused

Who is your greatest hero of all time?
Che Guevara

What's the most outrageous thing you've ever done?
I was out with Ryan Dunn one night during the rally and managed to get myself arrested whilst naked. I was 30 foot up a pole in Larry Flynt's strip club in New Orleans!

What was your worst moment on the Gumball?
Surviving on just 15 minutes of sleep every night

What was your best moment on the Gumball?
The other 23 hours and 45 minutes of each day

Who from history would be your dream Gumball co-driver?
Errol Flynn or Ghandi

Sum up your Gumball 3000 experience in one word?
Extraordinaryexpectularo

Q&A - ARCHERIO:

What is your ultimate Gumball car?
Chitty Chitty Bang Bang

What's your daily ride?
Roller skates (Bauer Turbo)

What's your favourite car related movie?
The Wrath

What's your favourite music?
Hip Hop and ABBA

What's your favourite clothing brand?
George at ASDA

What's your favourite magazine?
Razzle/ Escort

Who is your greatest hero of all time?
My uncle Miguel Mantovani

What's the most outrageous thing you've ever done?
Kissed a guy!

What was your worst moment on the Gumball?
Kissing a guy!

What was your best moment on the Gumball?
Kissing a guy!

Who from history would be your dream Gumball co-driver?
Roy Kinnear

Sum up your Gumball 3000 experience in one word?
Super-gay!

GUMBALLER PROFILE:

Name: MIGUEL MANTOVANI

Age: 53
Nationality: Cuban
Home Town: Holguin
Occupation: Entertainment Impresario
Career highlights: Singing at the opening of the 1952 Cuban Olympic games
Make of car driven in the Gumball: 2003 Ford F1-40 Truck, 2003 Rolls Royce Corniche
Special Modifications: Radar, rocket launcher, anti aircraft gun, 40 inch wheels, nitrous booster.

GUMBALLER PROFILE:

Name:

ARCHERIO MANTOVANI

Age: 19
Nationality: Cuban
Home Town: Havana
Occupation: Entertainer
Career highlights: MTV awards/ Radio 1 Glastonbury
Make of car driven in the Gumball:
Convertible Corniche Rolls Royce
Special Modifications: Sweets and heated seats

GUMBALLER PROFILE:

Name:

CLEMENTE RODRIGUEZ

Age: 57
Nationality: Cuban
Home Town: Havana
Occupation: Disc Jockey
Career highlights: Working with my family
Make of car driven in the Gumball: F350 (Ford Pick up)
Special Modifications: 95mph limiter
(To stop us winning!)

BO BRIDGES

J GOODWIN

Q&A - CLEMEMTE:

What is your ultimate Gumball car?
Ferrari Maranello

What's your daily ride?
Chopper (Raleigh)

What's your favourite car related movie?
Gumball 3000 "The Movie" or Cannonball Run

What's your favourite music?
Latin, Funk, Soul

What's your favourite clothing brand?
Guayabera shirts

What's your favourite magazine?
Attitude

Who is your greatest hero of all time?
Rock Hudson

What's the most outrageous thing you've ever done?
******** Ryan Dunn's ****

What was your worst moment on the Gumball?
Going home

What was your best moment on the Gumball?
Breakdancing in the Windsor Court Hotel New Orleans

Who from history would be your dream Gumball co-driver?
Freddie Mercury

Sum up your Gumball 3000 experience in one word?
Yeeeeeeeeeeeeeehah!!!

Above: Miguel; "How many miles to Havana? 98, you inquisitive little b**tard...!"

WORDSEARCH

Find the words in the grid before the cops catch up with our intrepid gumballers!

JOHNNYKNOXVILLE	FORDTORINO	SPEEDING	TICKETS
SANFRANCISCO	RYANDUNN	PORSCHE	MOVIE
LAMBORGHINI	CAREYHART	JACKASS	MIAMI
MAXIMILLION	GUMBALL	FERRARI	FAST

JOIN THE GUMBALL CLUB!

To receive your Gumball 3000 members goodie pack with all this stuff, fill in the form and send a cheque for £6.99 to Gumball 3000, 4, Lucerne Mews, London, W8 4ED.
Please make cheques payable to "Gumball 3000 Merchandise Ltd".

iron-on patch

postcards

stickers

top trumps

tax disc holder

GB300004

Please write in black ink and capital letters.
Please note the shaded boxes are for official use only.

1

G3/03 GUMBALL 3000 CLUB MEMBERSHIP

Join the Gumball 3000 Membership Club to receive news and updates of all Gumball 3000 events, films, and products. Your comments and answers to the questions will help us build up a profile of our Club Members, and once a month 10 members will randomly win a Gumball 3000 goody bag of T-shirts, stickers, and Top Trumps

Male ☐ Female ☐ Age ☐

Forenames _____

Surname _____

Address _____

Address _____

Post Town/City _____

State/County _____

Zip/Postcode _____

Country _____

Telephone Number _____

Cell/Mobile Number _____

Email Address _____

Nationality _____

Occupation _____

1. What is the ultimate Gumball car? _____

2. What is your favorite car movie? _____

3. What is your favorite driving music? _____

4. What is you favorite clothing brand? _____

5. What is the best car magazine available? _____

6. Other comments _____

For a limited period only, whilst stocks last.

Q&A:

What is your ultimate Gumball car?
2004 F60 Ferrari

What's your daily ride?
**2002 Custom Mercedes S500
& 2000 Custom Ford Expedition**

What's your favourite car related movie?
RAD

What's your favourite music?
Classic Rock

What's your favourite clothing brand?
Zoo York

What's your favourite magazine?
Anything with me in it ..... Ha Ha Ha

What's the most outrageous thing you've ever done?
You can't ask me that, I'm too gnarly!

What was your worst moment on the Gumball?
Waking up in the morning, and having a to drive with a dipshit blowing his horn, when he belonged in the circus.

What was your best moment on the Gumball?
Leaving the same Son of a Bitch in Arizona on the side of the road!

Who from history would be your dream Gumball co-driver?
Supermodel Giselle

Sum up your Gumball 3000 experience in one word?
HOLLA!!!!!!!

SUPERMAN!

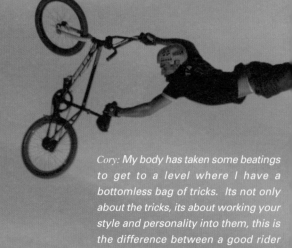

MOMENTUMPHOTO.COM

Cory: My body has taken some beatings to get to a level where I have a bottomless bag of tricks. Its not only about the tricks, its about working your style and personality into them, this is the difference between a good rider and a nasty rider!

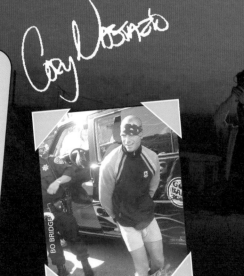

BO BRIDGES

GUMBALLER PROFILE:

Name:

CORY 'NASTY' NASTAZIO

Age: 25
Nationality: American
Home Town: Flushing, New York
Occupation: Pro BMX Rider
Career highlights: Gold Medal in Australia 2002, Robbed for 1st (took 2nd) in 2000 US X Games, Buying Mom the car of her dreams, seeing my bank account 2 years ago, Pulling my first Double Backflip, Best time, was Gumball 3000.
Car Driven in the Gumball: Jesse James Euro Van

GUMBALLER PROFILE:

Name:

TYLER EVANS

Age: 23
Nationality: American
Home Town: Canyon Lake, California
Occupation: Professional Athlete
Career highlights: Being alive
Make of car driven in the Gumball:
Jesse James Euro Van

Tyler Evans started riding at the tender age of 5, and rode his professional debut in 1996. Even the most basic of mathematics will tell you that Tyler spent his time wisely during those eleven years, and since his debut he is now held in high esteem by the Moto X community.

Recently returning to the race track after a year out to fine tune his freestyle skills, Tyler's pulling more tricks, getting more air and riding better than ever, hopefully silencing his critics and enabling him to concentrate more on what he does best.

Q&A:

What is your ultimate Gumball car?
Lamborghini Diablo
What's your daily ride?
Escalade/2003 Mercedes Benz
What's your favourite car related movie?
None
What's your favourite music?
Rap
What's your favourite clothing brand?
One Punch clothing
What's your favourite magazine?
Dub magazine
Who is your greatest hero of all time?
Scarface
What's the most outrageous thing you've ever done?
It changes every day
What was your worst moment on the Gumball?
Getting left in New Orleans
What was your best moment on the Gumball?
Not going to jail
Who from history would be your dream Gumball co-driver?
John Gotti
Sum up your Gumball 3000 experience in one word?
Sick

EVANS

BO BRIDGES

LOUISIANA
STATE POLICE

BO BRIDGES

Above: Tyler makes new friends!

T. EVANS

AMERICAN MUSCLE

★★★★★★★★★★★★★★

The featured Torino No. 178, was driven by Mr Guts, (aka Kevin Mikelonis). It was kitted out with every imaginable gadget and modified just enough to give the supercars a run for their money!

The Ford Torino is probably best known for it's dramatic tyre screeching turns and the driver's bonnet sliding antics on television sets throughout the 70's and 80's in the cult detective show, Starsky and Hutch. But despite being on home turf, the Ford Torino was one of just a handful of American Muscle Cars that entered the 2003 Gumball rally.

Popular for its no-nonsense styling and undeniably aggressive look, this car is more sought after today than it has ever been. In recent years the Torino has well and truly established itself firmly amongst the ranks of Classic Car aficionados the world over, and judging by the amount of heads this car turned between San Francisco and Miami, it will still be on many a car fanatic's wish list for many a year to come.

THE CAR IS THE STAR!!!

1972 FORD TORINO

Max speed (mph):	146
0-60 (seconds):	4.86
Max power (bhp):	430
Miles per gallon (mpg):	12
Engine capacity (cc):	351
Cost when new:	$4,314
Total produced:	3814
Gumball Factor:	68%

"Starsky and Hutch drove one of these American Beasts"

Above: Modifications included, satellite navigation, GPS, CB Radio, wireless Internet, and even a camera in a dummy rear pipe!

KEVIN MIKELONIS

STICKERS FOR YOUR RIDE!

The last checkpoint before reaching the Miami finish line was the 'delightfully tacky, yet unrefined' Hooters restaurant in Ocala, Florida. Drivers grabbed a quick bite to eat, (or a couple of girls), before hitting the road for the final leg.

Above: 'Delightfully tacky yet unrefined!'

Left: Gumball veterans Dimitry, Bucky and Shane get exited when they see even more Hooters girls!

JOE WINDSOR WILLIAMS

NICK THOMSON

Below: Uninterested, the girls look at the camera whilst Bucky tells them about himself!

MIKE SHARTIS

checkpoint

HOOTERS

NO ONE CAN PARTY LIKE I CAN!

BO BRIDGES

One time winner of the coveted "Spirit of the Gumball" accolade, Shane cemented his status as a Gumball legend following his colourful performance in the 2001 Rally shown on BBC1's Ruby Wax show and MTV's Jackass. Johnny Knoxville has since quoted Shane to be his "ultimate hero"

THE CAR IS THE STAR!!!

2002 MINI COOPER

Max speed (mph):	125
0-60 (seconds):	9.2
Max power (bhp):	115
Miles per gallon (mpg):	42.2
Engine capacity (cc):	1598
Cost when new:	$21,850
Total produced:	n/a
Gumball Factor:	52%

"No one can argue that this mini hasn't had an adventure!"

BO BRIDGES

Above: Always number 69, Shane is one of the few individuals to have taken part in every Gumball!

STUART SINGER

Shane: "Last year I got 11 tickets, and I didn't pay for any one of them. I just rolled them up a threw them out the f**king window"

TOM OLDHAM

LN02 EJO

GUMBALLER PROFILE:

Name:

SHANE SLEVIN

Age: 60
Nationality: Irish
Home Town: London
Occupation: Art Dealer
Career highlights: Meeting Andy Warhol
Make of car driven in the Gumball: Mini Cooper

RAGING BULLS!

★★★★★★★★★★★★★★★★★

This years Gumball saw a plethora of Lamborghini's take part, from the 70's classic Jalpa modified to a ridiculous 900bhp, to Diablo's in every shape and form including one with a 'nitro's' boost, taking the car to a top speed of 240mph!

The latest Lambo to come from the Italian stable, the stunning Murcielago, was also present with abundance. You'll hear the roar of it's 6.2 litre V12 engine before you even see it your mirrors, and there aren't too many cars on the road that can boast that claim to fame.

The 2003 Murcielago's closest rivals include the Aston Martin DB7 Vantage, the Ferrari 575M, and the Porsche 911 Turbo, and with such an impressive array of stable mates, you simply cannot fail to be impressed by this most desirable of cars.

In short, the Murcielago firmly puts the 'super' back into super cars. A worthy successor to the infamous Diablo, it goes like a bat out of hell that would leave Meatloaf crying into his leather waistcoat!

Above: Eyhab's Lambo handles like its on rails!

THE CAR IS THE STAR!!!

2003 LAMBORGHINI MURCIELAGO

Max speed (mph):	205
0-60 (seconds):	3.6
Max power (bhp):	580
Miles per gallon (mpg):	11
Engine capacity (cc):	6192
Cost when new:	$195,000
Total produced:	n/a
Gumball Factor:	94%

"Goes like a bat out of hell"

NICK THOMSON

Above: Nitros tanks in a Diablo...Scary!!

Above: A 900bhp Jalpa!!

Above: A yellow Diablo VT

CRAIG EARNSHAW

Below: Maximillion's Murcielago on the starting grid

Above: A 2002 Diablo 6.0

dress the gumballers

This is the lovely Gumballer and SuperModel Miss Jodie Kidd. Here for you to dress and undress again and again with our Gumball merchandise. If you wish to view them in more detail or purchase any of these items please visit our website @ www.gumball3000.com

"gives you balls" T-shirt

Hooded sweatshirt

TechnoMarine Limited Edition Watch

Racing Jacket - black with gold lining

Domed belt buckle

Whilst over here we have our Gumball die-hard, Shane 'the legend' Slevin. As you can see Shane is somewhat phased at the close proximity of Miss Kidd (with very little on). He does not seem overly worried that we kept the clothes for Jodie as they look so much better on her. He did refuse however to take off the jewelry along with his socks, so to help him warm up a bit we let him try on a some hats.

Bling bling gold medallion

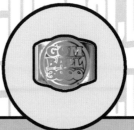

Bling bling gold ring

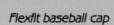

Flexfit baseball cap

Davida Classic Gumball Helmet

Royal Elastics racing boots - black

We have an ever growing list of merchandise available via the web site and at selected retailers. Products include: Gold medallion; Skater key chain; Gold ring; Belt buckle; Baseball caps; Davida Classic Gumball Helmets (full and pudding styles); Sweat-bands; a range of T-shirts; Hooded tops; Racing Jacket; Royal Elastics racing boots; Car badge; Top Trumps and the much anticipated " TechnoMarine " Limited Edition watch.

shop@ www.gumball3000.com

MIAMI, HERE WE COME!

After 3000 miles, through 9 states; having suffered 14 arrests and over $50,000 in fines, for 120 of the original 145 cars that left San Francisco the finish line is in sight.

Above: Miami is in sight!!

Above: 187 miles south lies the end party in Miami.

Above: Another silver Porsche!

Above: Lasek, DeAnda, Carrillo head for the Turnpike!

Above: Prowler heads to Miami...

Above: Doughnuts at the finish line in Miami.

Above: Bentley in Miami   Below inset: Mandarin Oriental at night   Below: Miami Parking lot!

checkpoint

MIAMI

BLING! BLING!

Above: ...And the 2003 Spirit of the Gumball trophy goes to Alex Roy and David Maher!

Right: A happy Rob Kenworthy holds his prize aloft!

Ryan Dunn: "Everybody get pissed drunk and f**k each other"

Above: Miguel and Archerio party into the early hours...

Above: Bo Bridges and Alex 'Dr Evil' Roy bite on their Gold Gumball Medallions and clutch their well earned Gumball trophy's!

Miguel Montevani takes the stage at the Spirit of the Gumball Awards... "For me it's a very emotional time. There's been a lot of driving, no sleeping, many drinking... it's the most special event in the world. It has been extraordinary"

SPIRIT OF GUMBALL!

Alex Roy and his co-pilot David Maher won the highly coveted 2003 Spirit of Gumball Award in style. It's difficult to explain how you go about receiving this accolade. One year the winner might have been the driver with the most speeding tickets and the heaviest penalties. The next it might be awarded to the car that stopped the most to help Gumballers in distress, help deal with breakdowns or help the less experienced deal with the police or the language. This year the award went to Alex because of the effort he put into making everyone smile.

2000 BMW M5 - Conversion
Deutsche Autobahn Polizei Verfolgung
(German Highway Patrol Pursuit)
Whelen Blue/Yellow Undercover Beacons (x2)
Autobahn Polizei Uniforms (x2)
Doctor's Uniforms (x2) + Inflatable Nurse
Dinan Stage 1 Engine Software
Kelleners Sport Exhaust
Valentine 1 Laser/Radar Detector
Valentine 1 Concealed Display
Lidatek LE-2020 Laser Jammers (x2)
Uniden BC785D Digital Police Scanner
Uniden PRO520XL CB Radio
Garmin 2350 GPS Navigation System
Autotech Laser Diffuser Plates (x2)

Above: Partners in crime; Alex Roy and co-driver David Maher

Below: !Pursuit!

THE CAR IS THE STAR!!!

BMW M5 'POLIZEI'

Max speed (mph):	115
0-60 (seconds):	4.8
Max power (bhp):	394
Miles per gallon (mpg):	24
Engine capacity (cc):	4941
Cost when new:	$69,970
Total produced:	n/a
Gumball Factor:	86%

"Modified to take on the world!"

Above: She never complained once!

JOE WINDSOR WILLIAMS

Q&A:

What is your ultimate Gumball car?
2005 Ford GT, Vector W12

What's your daily ride?
2000 BMW M5, 1987 Porsche 911 Targa, 1996 Porsche 911 Targa, 2003 Subaru WRX Sti

What's your favourite car related movie?
Rendezvous, Ronin

What's your favourite music?
Industrial/Techno/Metal

What's your favourite clothing brand?
The house brand on the Death Star

What's your favourite magazine?
Evo, Der New Yorker, Der New York Observer

Who is your greatest hero of all time?
Neil Armstrong - first man on the Moon

What's the most outrageous thing you've ever done?
Ven I told the Texas Autobahn Polizei "Dis BMW Autobahn Polizei Verfolgung M5 von Munchen vaz donated to der NYPD to raize der money fur die 9/11 viktims aus testicular cancer driving im der Gumball Rally - may ve take your picture?"

What was your worst moment on the Gumball?
Running out auf der petrol, tvize!

What was your best moment on the Gumball?
Ven ve used der Polizei licht to stoppen Herr Tony Hawk im der Dodge Viper!

Who from history would be your dream Gumball co-driver?
Sophia Loren

Sum up your Gumball 3000 experience in one word?
Indescribable!

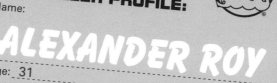

GUMBALLER PROFILE:

Name:

ALEXANDER ROY

Age: 31
Nationality: American
Home Town: New York City
Occupation: Writer/Producer/Director
Career highlights: The New York Guerilla Grand Prix
Make of car driven in the Gumball: 2000 BMW M5
Special modifications: Far too many to list here!

CROSSWORD

ACROSS

3) British Aero 8 (6)

6) Tyler Evans' Favourite Hero (8)

8) Gumball organisers last name (6)

9) Ryan Dunn's daily ride (8)

13) Tina Basich's home town (10)

14) Tara Dakides rides one of these (9)

16) Jesse James's favourite music (6)

17) Tara Dakides' hero (8)

18) Spirit of Gumball (4,3)

19) Fastest car on rally (10)

DOWN

1) Naked Brothers (5)

2) Supermodels favourite film (7,3)

4) Russian car transporter (8)

6) Har Mar _____ (9)

7) Cuban tailor (10)

10) Driver for Team Yoo Hoo (5,5)

11) Hungover Skater (5,5)

12) Carey's signature (4,6)

15) Pastrana's fave magazine (6)

10) Drove a Dodge Viper (5,4)

HAR MAR SUPERSTAR!

Q&A:

What is your ultimate Gumball car?
Some sort of three-wheeled motor-tricycle or just a sidecar

What's your daily ride?
I haven't driven since I moved to London, but I'm a geek who likes Hondas and Toyotas

What's your favourite car related movie?
Cannonball Run

What's your favourite music?
R&B and rock

What's your favourite clothing brand?
Paul Frank

What's your favourite magazine?
Dazed and Confused

Who is your greatest hero of all time?
Stevie Wonder

What's the most outrageous thing you've ever done?
No idea

What was your worst moment on the Gumball?
When the sound guy in Miami threw me down the stairs because I had dropped his $50 microphone

What was your best moment on the Gumball?
I got to out-run a cop who was trying to arrest me for lewdness when I accidentally exposed myself. I wish I could have done the whole race. (Har Mar flew in to present the awards on the last night in Miami.)

Who from history would be your dream Gumball co-driver?
Dom DeLouise from the original Cannonball Run

Sum up your Gumball 3000 experience in one word?
Party!

Described as 'The Dirtiest man in Rock', Har Mar Superstar is something of a phenomenon. Regularly found sweating on stages around the world wearing nothing but a pair of out-sized Y-front underpants, swigging from a bottle of champagne and crooning into a microphone, Har Mar Superstar really does have to be seen to be believed.

Love him or hate him, you can't fail to be...amazed by his high energy, rawkus and quite simply outrageous performances. Fellas, lock up your wives/ girlfriends/ daughters, Har Mar Superstar has entered the building!

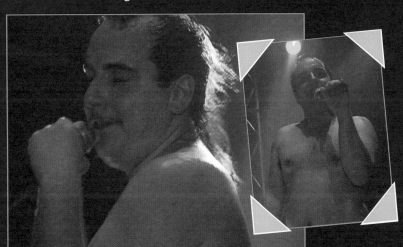

GUMBALLER PROFILE:

Name: **HAR MAR SUPERSTAR**

Age: 25

Nationality: American

Home Town: Minneapolis

Occupation: Rocker

Career highlights: Dueting with Andy Taylor from Duran Duran. Residency at Manumission in Ibiza. Touring with the Strokes. Traveling the world and having my music pay for it

Make of car driven in the Gumball: No car. I fly, fools!

Special Modifications: It was an airplane, and I flew first class. That's REALLY special.

JONATHAN BUSHELL

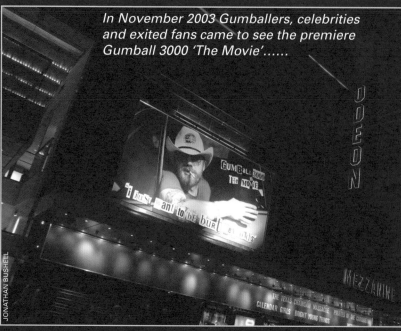

In November 2003 Gumballers, celebrities and exited fans came to see the premiere Gumball 3000 'The Movie'......

JONATHAN BUSHELL

Above: **Black and gold Gumball carpet!**

Above: **Gumball 3000 'The Movie' Premiere at the Odeon Leicester Square, London**

MICHAEL TOMLINSON

MICHAEL TOMLINSON

Above: **Supermodel Landi makes her entrance**

Above: **Max, Julie, Angie and Ryan Dunn**

Above: Head-spin world champion Archerio busts a move!

Above: Jodie Marsh and Porn legend Ron Jeremy

Above: Viva la Bam!

Above: Nick Moran of Lock Stock fame

SCOTT PLANE

ANTONIO ALVENDIA

ANTONIO ALVENDIA

ANTONIO ALVENDIA

Above Left to Right: Ryan Dunn and Angie, Cory Nastazio with girlfriend, The Rawlings "Gumball Rocks" family outing!

In February 2004, Gumball 3000 'The Movie' premiered at the famous Mann's Chinese Theatre on Hollywood Boulevard, before it's nationwide cinema release across the USA.

ANTONIO ALVENDIA, www.ciphergarage.com

GUMBALL 3000
THE MOVIE

SPEED LIMIT 55

NARRATED by BURT REYNOLDS

GUMBALL 3000

GUMBALL 3000 FILMS PRESENT A GIANT FILM AND TV PRODUCTION "GUMBALL 3000" THE MOVIE NARRATED BY BURT REYNOLDS
DIRECTED BY STEVEN GREEN EDITED BY CHRIS SHAW PRODUCED BY DAVID GREEN EXECUTIVE PRODUCERS MAXIMILLION COOPER JULIE BRANGSTRUP & ARTHUR CHIRKINIAN GRAPHIC DESIGN MIKE LAWRENCE
MUSIC SUPERVISOR MARC ROBINSON MUSIC BY UNIVERSAL & NINJATUNE SOUNDTRACK AVAILABLE ON UNIVERSAL MUSIC THE GUMBALL 3000 RALLY IS A REAL EVENT 6 DAYS 150 CARS 3000 MILES CREATED BY MAXIMILLION COOPER

On a clear day in April, 150 cars set off on an adventure of a lifetime, racing 3000 miles from San Francisco to Miami. We pick up on the action three hours into the race as the cars head for Las Vegas...

THE ADVENTURES OF CAPTAIN GUMBALL

EPISODE 1

CO-STARRING DR.EVIL AND HIS BLONDES

WITH MAX GAZILLION$

AND WITH A SPECIAL GUEST APPEARANCE FROM THE LEGENDARY...

...BURT REYNOLDS

LIVE ON AIR

WELCOME BACK RACE FANS. THE ACTIONS HOTING UP AS CURRENT LEADER DR.EVIL IS THE FIRST TO BE PULLED OVER. THAT SERVES HIM RIGHT FOR LETTING DOWN THE TIRES OF HIS CLOSEST RIVALS.

SOMEWHERE IN NEVADA...

HAVE SOME $$$ PEASANTS.

...MAX GAZILLION$ TAKES THE LEAD

MEANWHILE,

DR.EVIL YOU'RE UNDER ARREST FOR SPEEDING.

IT WON'T BE LONG BEFORE DR.EVIL HAS CHARMED HIS WAY OUT OF TROUBLE.

HEY OFFICER, YOU CAN KEEP ONE OF MY BLONDES IF YOU LET ME GO!!

OK DR.EVIL YOU CAN GO. I'LL TAKE THE TALL, PRETTY ONE. HAVE A NICE DAY !!

MEANWHILE, BACK ON THE ROAD, OUR RANDOM HERO CAPT. GUMBALL APPEARS TO BE CATCHING MAX GAZILLIONS

YOU CAN'T BUY ME GAZILLIONS.

SO LONG GAZILLIONS, SEE YOU IN MIAMI !!

GOD'AMN HE'S FAST!!

NEVADA STATE POLICE

UNDETERRED BY GAZILLIONS' $$$, CAPT.GUMBALL PUTS HIS FOOT DOWN.

FOCUSED ON WINNING CAPT.GUMBALL DIDN'T NOTICE THE THE COP CAR ON THE ROADSIDE...

SECONDS LATER CAPT. GUMBALL SEES THE BLUE LIGHTS IN HIS MIRROR.

WHAT SHALL I DO? PULL OVER AND LET GAZILLIONS TAKE THE LEAD, OR DO I TRY TO LOSE THIS COP?

IN A MOMENT OF MADNESS CAPTAIN GUMBALL SPEEDS UP 180MPH AND LEAVES THE COP BEHIND IN HIS DUST.

GOTTA GO FOR IT !!!

JUST AS THE COP CAR DISAPPEARED IN HIS REAR VIEW, CAPTAIN GUMBALL NOTICES TO HIS HORROR, A FULL ROAD BLOCK IN THE DISTANCE.

AT THAT MOMENT A DIRT TRACK APPEARS OFF INTO THE NAVAJO RESERVATION.

I'VE NEVER HEARD AN UNDER-CARRIAGE GET MORE BEAT UP, OFF-ROADING AT FRICKIN' 80MPH.

COPS

I KNOW !!!

WITH THE COPS IN HOT PUSUIT, JUST WHEN YOU THINK THINGS COULDN'T GET ANY WORSE THE DIRT ROAD ENDS AT A CANYON.

IT'S THE END OF THE ROAD, WHAT SHOULD I DO ?!?

WITH OUR HERO DOOMED HE TAKES THE CAR INTO THE TREES AND HIDES IN THE BUSHES FOR FEAR OF THE POLICE FINDING HIM...

IF THE POLICE CATCH ME I'LL GET A YEAR IN JAIL !

IS THIS THE END OF THE RACE FOR OUR HERO, OR WILL HE MAKE A MIRACULOUS RECOVERY?

MEANWHILE BACK IN THE RACE, WILL MAX GAZILLION$ $$$ RUN OUT BEFORE THE FINSH, OR WILL DR.EVIL COME GOOD?.

NO ONE CAN CATCH ME, I'M TOO RICH !!

FIND OUT IN THE NEXT EPISODE OF... THE ADVENTURES OF CAPTAIN GUMBALL. ...TO BE CONTINUED.

6 Ferrari F50 Spider

...signed to commemorate Ferrari's 50th ...niversary.

SPECIFICATION

Max Speed (mph)	202
0-60 (seconds)	3.7
Max Power (bhp)	520
Miles per gallon (mpg)	8
Engine capacity (cc)	4699
Cost when new	$480,000
Total produced (lowest wins)	349
Gumball Factor	98%

2002   A wolf in wolf's clothing!

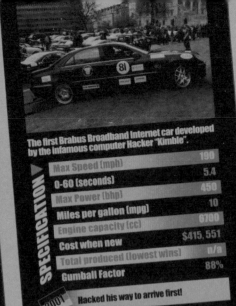

The first Brabus Broadband Internet car developed by the infamous computer Hacker "Kimble".

SPECIFICATION

Max Speed (mph)	190
0-60 (seconds)	5.4
Max Power (bhp)	450
Miles per gallon (mpg)	10
Engine capacity (cc)	6700
Cost when new	$415,551
Total produced (lowest wins)	n/a
Gumball Factor	88%

2001   Hacked his way to arrive first!

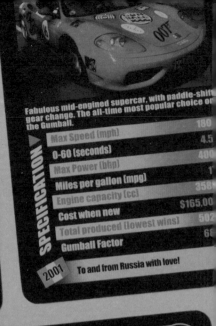

Fabulous mid-engined supercar, with paddle-shift gear change. The all-time most popular choice of the Gumball.

SPECIFICATION

Max Speed (mph)	180
0-60 (seconds)	4.5
Max Power (bhp)	400
Miles per gallon (mpg)	1
Engine capacity (cc)	358
Cost when new	$165,00
Total produced (lowest wins)	502
Gumball Factor	6

2001   To and from Russia with love!

---

2 Silver Arrow Ferrari 512 LM

Commissioned in 2000 as a 'one-off' to take part in the Gumball. This unique supercar is 'barely' legal to drive on public streets.

SPECIFICATION

Max Speed (mph)	210
0-60 (seconds)	3.8
Max Power (bhp)	560
Miles per gallon (mpg)	8
Engine capacity (cc)	4942
Cost when new	$480,000
Total produced (lowest wins)	1
Gumball Factor	96%

2000   When I win the lotto!

Thank You!

Every effort has been made to credit the images correctly. Please don't cry if we have missed the mark, it was and is never our intention to hurt anyone's feelings. Thank you also to anyone who helped, no matter how small his or her part in making this annual get out of the starting blocks and into your hands. Keep an eye out in the shops for the next annual coming this Autumn.

1973 Ferrari GTB 4 'Daytona'

Known as the 'Daytona' because of Ferrari's overwhelming victory in the Daytona endurance race in the late 1960's.

SPECIFICATION

Max Speed (mph)	173
0-60 (seconds)	6.1
Max Power (bhp)	352
Miles per gallon (mpg)	12
Engine capacity (cc)	4390
Cost when new	n/a
Total produced (lowest wins)	128
Gumball Factor	85%

1999   A Gumball essential!

Chrysler Dodge Viper GTS

...blast power and devilish good looks that strike ...in the hearts of even the bravest of men.

Max Speed (mph)	177

2002 Morgan Aero 8

The first new Morgan in over 30 years earned its stripes under the right foot of Charles Morgan on 4 consecutive rallies.

Max Speed (mph)	160
0-60 (seconds)	4.9
Max Power (bhp)	286

2003 Lamborghini Murcielago

The latest thoroughbred to emerge from the Lamborghini stable is a worthy successor to the Diablo.

Max Speed (mph)	205
0-60 (seconds)	3.6
Max Power (bhp)	560
Miles per gallon (mpg)	11